ALPINISM

by

PETER CLIFF

Mike.

With many thanks for
you help with this book
— and for such a good
job.

Pete.   May '98

© PETER CLIFF 1998

First Edition 1998

ISBN 1 871890 09 8

FRONT COVER: on the Gran Zebru 3851m. Ortler.

Distributed by Cordee, 3A de Montfort Street, Leicester, LE1 7HD

Printed by Highland Printers, 13 Henderson Road, Inverness.

INTRODUCTION

The move from British mountaineering to Alpinism can be a daunting experience. The routes are longer, the mountains are higher, there are glaciers and crevasses, thunderstorms and rockfall are more common.

Watching and copying others who appear to be knowledgeable can be useful, but some are not as knowledgeable as they appear.

This book addresses the crucial issues which are essential to safe Alpinism, whether walking or climbing. It does not claim to be the authoritative book on all the issues. For that you must go to the standard books on the subjects and some ideas are listed in the Bibliography.

ACKNOWLEDGMENTS

Many of the ideas in this book, indeed the very concept of the book, originate from the work I have done with the Jonathan Conville Alpine Courses. I thank the students, the Trustees and my fellow guides (who may recognise some of their own ideas within these pages).

Mike Anderson for the diagrams.
Nick Banks for checking the text.
Eric Pirie for help with the illustrations.

BIBLIOGRAPHY

The following books are recommended for further reading on specific topics:

Albisser P   *Précis de Météorolgie pour Alpinistes*
               (in French)

Barry J   *Snow and Ice Climbing*

Cliff P   *Mountain Navigation*

Daffern T   *Avalanche Safety for Skiers and Climbers*

Fyffe + Peter *The Handbook of Climbing*

Müller W   *Alpinisme d' été (*in French*)*

Pedgley D   *Mountain Weather*

Schubert P   *Die Anwendung des Seiles* (in German)

Shepherd N   *Self Rescue Techniques*

Thomas M   *Weather for Hillwalkers + Climbers*

THE AUTHOR

Peter Cliff is an International Mountain Guide. For several years he has been Director of Training for the Jonathan Conville Trust which provides subsidised training courses in the Alps and Scotland.

He has written three other books: *Mountain Navigation*, *Ski Mountaineering* and *A Guidebook to the Haute Route*.

CONTENTS

The North Ridge of Piz Badile

ABSEILING

The two occasions you are likely to abseil are:

- a multi-pitch abseil as part of a descent.
- over a bergschrund which is too big to jump.

MULTI-PITCH ABSEILS

Abseil Points - On the popular routes the abseil points will be in place and will consist of pegs, bolts or slings round blocks. The pegs and bolts may be linked by a chain, hopefully with a great big ring or mail-lon through which you pass the ropes.

If slings are in place and you are in doubt about their strength, back them up with your own. For this it is normal to carry a length of light rope (5.5mm or 6mm) and a knife. The traditional view is that UV light damages nylon, but recent tests suggest that this is not such a major concern.

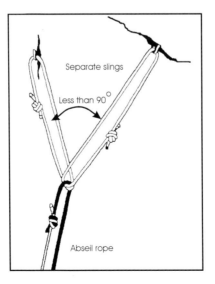

THE SLINGS SHOULD MAKE AN ANGLE WITH THE ANCHOR POINTS OF LESS THAN 90° , AND THE ABSEIL ROPES SHOULD BE THREADED THROUGH THE SLINGS IN SUCH A WAY THAT, IF ONE ANCHOR FAILS, THE ROPES ARE STILL IN THE REMAINING ONE.

Joining Knot - If the route is a popular low-grade one, the abseil points may be 25 metres apart, because the assumption will be that many parties will be climbing on a single 50m rope. But for all other routes the assumption will be that double ropes are being used, and the abseil points will be 50m apart.

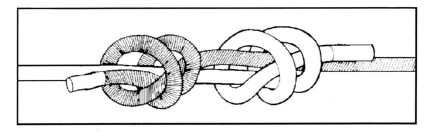

THE DOUBLE FISHERMAN'S IS THE TRADITIONAL KNOT FOR JOINING THE ROPES.

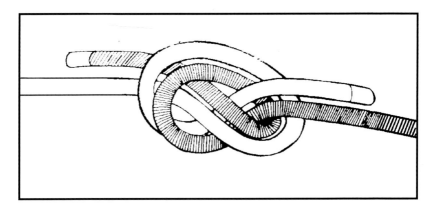

THE OVERHAND KNOT IS BETTER. IT IS QUICKER TO TIE, IT RUNS OVER EDGES BETTER AND IS LESS LIKELY TO CATCH WHEN YOU PULL THE ROPES THROUGH.

MAKE SURE THAT THE TAILS ARE AT LEAST 1" OR 30 CMS LONG.

Abseiling

- abseil smoothly and carefully, checking that the screwgate remains done up.

- if you are abseiling into the unknown, it is worth tying an overhand in the ends of the ropes so that you don't abseil off the ends of the ropes. But this takes extra time and is by no means recommended practice every time you abseil.

- it will be important to know which rope to pull, as you don't want to pull the knot through the abseil anchor with a risk of it jamming. The last person to abseil can do this by clipping a quickdraw onto that rope, so marking it.

- for a serious abseil it is worth using a prusik. It is time consuming to put on (and speed is important) so it is not recommended as standard practice. The prusik can be either above or below the abseiling device.

A PRUSIK BELOW THE ABSEILING DEVICE, CLIPPED INTO A LEG LOOP; IN THIS WAY YOUR CONTROLLING HAND TAKES DOWN THE PRUSIK AND YOUR OTHER HAND IS FREE FOR PUSHING OFF ETC.

Reaching the next abseil point

- Lock-off the abseil device and attach yourself with a sling to the abseil point.

- as your partner abseils down, hold the ropes so that you can check him if necessary.

- prepare a sling for your partner and clip him in when he arrives.

Pulling the ropes through

- before you start to pull them through, pass the end of the marked rope down through the new abseil point so there is no chance of losing the ropes.

- pull the marked one steadily holding your breath that they don't jam.

Jammed abseil ropes

- if the ropes are still through the abseil point above you and if you have both ropes in your hand, it's prusiking time. A good system is one short prusik for the body and another below that extended with a sling for your foot (see 'Crevasse Rescue').

- if you only have one rope or if they have cleared the abseil point above you, prusiking is out of the question. Having exhausted all attempts to free the ropes, the only option is to climb back up using the free end of rope as a climbing rope. Not much fun.

Abseiling over a Bergshrund

The anchor will probably be a snow bollard. It will be as well to reinforce it with the ice axes and the last person down brings the axes with him. (See "Snow and Ice Belays").

It may be that the bollard now fails, but you may still get away with it as your friends are on the downhill side of the bergschrund and you are attached to the ropes through your abseil device. If you have the presence of mind, you should grab hold of the ropes above the abseil device.

Young climber on the Petite Aiguille Verte, Chamonix.

ACCLIMATISATION

I am often asked: "How important is acclimatisation and how long would I need before doing, say, Mont Blanc ?" There is no definitive answer as there are a number of factors involved and each individual responds differently to each factor.

PHYSIOLOGICAL ISSUES

As we go higher, there is less oxygen available and the body starts to create more red cells in order to push around the available oxygen. This is the basic issue and sometimes a period of 10 - 14 days is mentioned as being needed for this process.

But then there is our own individual body, particularly our own level of fitness and our own ability to put up with pain and discomfort.

PSYCHOLOGICAL ISSUES

And there is more to it than these pure physiological issues. Coming straight from Britain, the Alps look so big - huge rockfaces, enormous glaciers with nasty big crevasses, snow slopes which go on for ever and which look so steep..... It takes a day or two to get used to this and in the meantime our performance will be something less than fluent, because we will be nervous.

SYMPTOMS

The symptoms of early altitude problems are:

- breathlessness
- feeling dizzy
- headache
- feeling sick
- being sick

It is not unusual to feel a bit breathless around 1,800m. And if the pressure drops with the weather, a headache might come on around 2,700m.

TREATMENT

Drink lots of water. If you have a headache, take an Aspirin or Paracetamol; and if the headache continues, drop height straight away. If you start to feel sick, drop height straight away.

ACCLIMATISING

If your aim is to climb Mont Blanc 4807m it is best to start with modest altitude objectives around 3,700m, sleeping around 2,500 - 2,700m. Build it up in a steady progression to 4,000 - 4,300m peaks. All the time your body will be adjusting, you will be gaining in fitness, you will be getting used to the big mountains, and you will be sorting out your systems with you rucsack and equipment.

Throughout, make sure you drink a lot of water. Some like to drink through the day; others don't like to carry the weight but drink a lot when they get back to the hut or valley. Watch the colour of your urine: light yellow is right, dark yellow means it's time to go to the water tap and stick your mouth round it.

> **TOP TIP: When abseiling, always clip into the new abseil point.**

> **TOP TIP: Drink lots of water**

AREAS

The Alps straddle several countries - France, Switzerland, Austria, Italy and Germany. There are numerous areas for climbing and walking, each area having its own character. Part of the enjoyment of Alpinism is planning the holiday and then discovering a new area and culture. But as a novice Alpinist you will hear the main areas talked about and the following brief notes might help your choice.

AROLLA - a small village in Switzerland to the west of Zermatt. The village itself has maintained as unspoilt character, while offering all the facilities an Alpinist needs.

- excellent rock climbing.
- reasonable straightforward glaciers.
- easy peaks at PD/AD.

BERNESE OBERLAND - a very high glaciated area with such famous names as the Eiger and Jungfrau. Long walks in, unless you use the Jungfrau railway.

- big glaciers, some quite serious.
- high mountains with many PD routes.

BREGALIA - in eastern Switzerland close to the Italian border. One of the most popular areas among British climbers after Chamonix.

- excellent rock climbs on superb granite, many long routes.
- equally good mixed routes.

CHAMONIX - the most popular area for British climbers, but not the best for novices as much of it is serious.

- rock climbing at all altitudes, much of it on excellent granite.
- mixed routes of top quality and grades.
- glaciers vary from easy to very hard.

DAUPHINE - a wonderful area in a National Park. Quite big and serious.

- excellent rock climbing.
- quite crevassed glaciers.
- some good peaks at easier grades and many harder routes.

DOLOMITES - a stunning area in the eastern Alps.

- no major glaciers.
- rock climbing of all grades and lengths,invariably on excellent rock.
- via ferratas (these are exciting routes up improbable ways made safe by fixed cables and ladders).

OTZTAL/STUBAI - these two areas are in western Austria and have everything for the novice Alpinist.

- easy glaciers linking some of the best huts in the Alps.
- peaks below 4,000m with easy routes at PD/AD.
- not renowned for the rock climbing, but some good rock on the mixed routes.

SAAS FEE - including the villages of Saas Grund and Saas Almagell, this has everything for a novice Alpinist.

- some easy glaciers, others more serious.
- medium altitude rock routes at easier grades.
- 4,000m peaks with routes from easy to very hard.

ZERMATT - features the most famous mountain in the world - the Matterhorn. Teaming with visitors, banks and now a MacDonalds.

- many of the glaciers are serious.
- lots of 4,000m peaks, many with easy routes at PD/AD.

AVALANCHES, ROCKFALL, ICEFALL

AVALANCHES

The two main avalanches of concern to the summer Alpinist are wet loose snow and slabs.

LOOSE SNOW AVALANCHES

It is not unusual for it to snow down to 2,500m (even 2,000m), early in the season, say the beginning of July. That could put a lot of snow down at altitudes over 3,500m.It is then quite normal to get some good weather with hot temperatures. Over 4,000m it is likely to stay freezing, but between 3,200m - 3,700m the sun may melt the snow starting on SE/S aspect slopes at around 10.30hrs and getting onto the W aspect slopes in the early afternoon.

The snowmelt starts with a little bit of snow falling off steep rocks. As it falls it dislodges more snow which is already melted and ready to go. This takes more, and so the avalanche develops.

Loose snow avalanches start from a single point and fan out. The snow is wet from the melting of the sun which means that when the avalanche comes to a halt, the debris is likely to set into very hard blocks. These avalanches are predictable because they are caused by two factors which we as mountaineers can observe: a snowfall, and the heat of the sun.

Loose snow

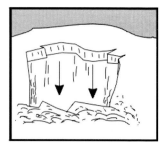

Windslab

WINDSLAB AVALANCHES

The windslab is as common as the loose snow avalanche, but is more difficult to predict.

Wind blowing over a mountain accelerates on the windward side of ridges and decelerates on the leeward. Snow is blown along the windward slopes and as this happens, the crystals get knocked about and lose their branches. When the wind decelerates on the lee slope, the snow is deposited as a slab. The hardness or softness of the slab depends on the wind strength, temperature and humidity.

The end result is that a slab of snow, anything from a few inches to several feet in depth, is deposited on top of the previous snow pack. In doing so, it may have little adhesion to the layer below.

Slab forms, therefore, on lee slopes. But rocky outcrops and gullies can cause eddies which in turn deposit slab on what are basically windward slopes.

And it need not necessarily be snowing at the time. A light breeze can blow snow around on a sunny day and deposit it as slab.

The snow may be dry or wet.

Dry

A dry slab avalanche will be either hard or soft slab. You can push your fist or boot into soft slab, but hard slab is so hard that one can walk on it. An unsuspecting mountaineer may flounder up some deep snow and then to his relief find that he has reached some hard snow that he can walk on. This hard snow could well be hard slab, and the mountaineer the trigger for the avalanche.

The debris of a soft slab avalanche looks very much like that of a loose snow avalanche, whereas that of hard slab normally consists of well-defined angular blocks of snow.

Wet

A wet slab avalanche is often a slow moving, enormous weight of dense wet snow with great destructive power, and which freezes to a solid mass when it stops.

Break-off

Whereas the loose snow starts from a single point and fans out as it descends, the slab starts with a well-defined fracture line. This fracture line forms an irregular and often arc shaped line across the top of the avalanche path with the face of fracture perpendicular to the slope.

Five Factors

For a windslab to start the following must be present:

(i) Steepness of slope: most slab avalanches are on slopes of between 30°-45°.

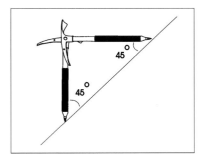

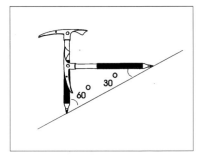

TWO AXES OF THE SAME LENGTH CAN BE USED TO MEASURE THE SLOPE ANGLE.

(ii) Aspect of slope: slab builds up on lee slopes; and so, subject to the vagaries of the local eddies, it will normally be found on the predominantly lee slopes.

(iii) Weak layer: somewhere in the snow pack there must be a weak layer, the most likely ones in summer being:

- sun crust which forms a good hard layer and any slab subsequently forming on it will have little adhesion to it.

- a layer of graupel, acting like a layer of ball bearings for any subsequent build-up of slab. Graupel is a snow crystal, heavily rimed and round in shape which looks like hail, but which is actually a snow crystal, and which often falls with a cold front.

- melting causes water to percolate down a slab of rock, breaking the adhesion of the snowpack with the rock.

(iv) Fracture along the top: a mountaineer traversing a slab may get quite a fright to suddenly see a small line appear across the snow. This may be enough to set the avalanche off, in which case it is the trigger of the avalanche. But often it does not actually go, in which case this line is what is known as a tension fracture.

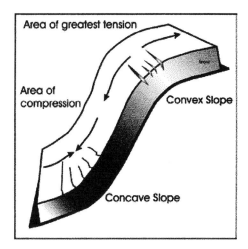

THE MOST LIKELY PLACE FOR A TENSION FRACTURE IS IN THE AREA OF GREATEST TENSION ON A CONVEX SLOPE.

(v) Trigger: the final trigger may be one of many things, e.g:

- a mountaineer traversing the slope. If he traverses well below the tension crack, the slab may break off above him putting him in a particularly bad position. If the slab breaks off under him, he may be able to put his ice axe in above him and hold himself there.

- any of the following may break off and fall onto the slab below: a cornice, a small loose snow avalanche, rockfall, ice breaking off from a hanging glacier.

- melting may weaken the bed surface.

ROCKFALL

There is a lot of loose rock in the Alps and every winter creates more - water gets into cracks, the water freezes, ice takes up more room than water so the ice expands and cracks the rocks. For the rest of the winter the ice holds the rocks in place, but the hot summer weather melts the snow and the ice, and then we get rockfall.

CAUSES OF ROCKFALL

Once the hot summer weather has melted the snow and ice, the scene is set and rockfall will happen given certain factors:

- specific warming of individual loose rocks e.g. by 10.00 hrs on SE/S aspects.

- if it has not frozen at night.

- heavy rainfall can get in behind rocks and dislodge them.

- careless people.

DANGER ZONES

If the situation is generally bad for rockfall, it has to be recognised that you could be hit wherever you are.

The danger increases:

- in gullies or couloirs, because many of the rocks will already be there or will fall into them.

- when below other people.

- on steep dry glaciers with rocks.

PRECAUTIONS

- alter your plans and avoid routes with gullies/couloirs; pick exposed ridges and routes known to have good rock.

- wear a helmet.

- watch the freezing level.

- ask for local advice from guides, guides' offices, hut guardians and other climbers.

ICE-FALL

An ice-fall occurs where the glacier drops down steeply so causing a lot of tension in the surface ice, resulting in a jumbled mass of crevasses and blocks of ice. The blocks of ice are called seracs. They are often very unstable and fall over due to gravity.

Ice can also fall from hanging glaciers. Due to gravity, lower sections progressively break away from the main part of the hanging glacier and eventually fall - often causing very large avalanches.

Since the main factor involved is gravity, ice can fall at any time - even when it is freezing at night. A lesser factor is the heat of the sun.

DANGER ZONES - below seracs and below hanging glaciers.

PRECAUTIONS

- wearing a helmet won't make much difference.

- do not go below seracs which look unstable.

- ask for local advice on your proposed route from guides, guides' offices, hut guardians and other climbers.

TOP TIP: avalanches kill climbers even in summer, so learn about them.

BIVOUACING

There are two main times when we bivouac.

LONG ROUTES

Many big Alpine routes require a bivouac, either on the ascent or the descent, or maybe both. By the time you get to doing these routes, you won't need the advice of this book. You will have discovered the need to travel as light as possible and your only concessions to the bivouac are likely to be:

- a group shelter or individual bivvy bag.
- an extra layer of clothing, e.g. down jacket.
- a small stove and pan to heat water for soup and tea.
- cold food.

The plan is to rest rather than to get a good night's sleep; and the main consideration is lightness balanced against the ability to rest (and survive a storm).

INSTEAD OF USING HUTS

I sometimes call this the 'impoverished British student bivouac' but that is being unfair to it (and to British students); and it should stand on its own feet because it has a lot going for it.

It may be that you are on a limited budget and the huts are too expensive. Or you may prefer the peace and quiet of the bivouac. Or perhaps there is no convenient hut.

THE LAW

In France the law is: we may only bivouac between the hours of sunset and sunrise. The French have a great ability to turn a blind eye to laws which seem at the moment to be inappropriate, so early in the season a couple of bivvy tents tucked away in a quiet corner may be ignored. But when it has gone too far, they sometimes use a measure of force which may come as something of a surprise if you are on the receiving end.

The advice is: collapse and cache your bivvy between the hours of sunrise and sunset.

METHOD

The idea will be to try and get some sleep and to eat reasonably, so you will probably wish to take:

- bivvy bag or outer skin of a tent.
- sleeping mat and sleeping bag.
- cooker and food.

ETHICAL CONSIDERATIONS

Many people bivouac very close to huts. This must detract from the pleasure of the bivouac, when part of the point is to get away from huts and people. But it is surely unethical on the grounds that you should not have the security which the huts offer, without contributing something to the costs of building and maintaining them.

Also, if you bivvy above the hut you may well pollute the hut's water supply: the first rainfall washes your waste (and that of other people who have 'gone' behind rocks above the hut) into the hut's water supply.

Notwithstanding these points, this second type of bivouac can be a great experience. But we should do it observing the local laws and well away from huts.

CHOICE OF ROUTE

When planning routes you might find it useful to think in terms of:
- technical.
- non-technical.

and to then split them again into:
- medium altitude.
- higher altitude.

TECHNICAL ROUTES

Technical routes may be pure rock climbs, or pure snow/ice climbs, or a mixture (mixed routes). As you start, begin with modest grades (say PD) at a modest altitude, building up your ability to move quickly on the great variety of terrain which is Alpinism.

You will discover that, while a PD may have short pitches of II and III, much of it will be on scrambling type ground where guidebook time requires you to move together. You will also discover that a lot of time is spent on loose rock, which requires a delicate touch - especially in your footwork.

If the first route goes well (i.e. you keep to guidebook time) you can then either put the grade up or go for a longer route at higher altitude - but not both at the same time.

NON-TECHNICAL ROUTES

These are either the bigger mountains by their easy routes, sometimes derisively dismissed as snow plods; or they may be glacier journeys.

Whichever, they are well worth doing because you will learn a lot about snow, ice and glaciers. You will learn about the weather from watching the changing patterns during the day. You will increase your fitness and acclimatisation. And all of this experience will stand you in good stead for the day you do a long route at altitude and have to descend one of these long snow routes or glaciers.

In unsettled weather it is best to keep off the technical routes, especially the longer ones at altitude; but it may be perfectly feasible to do, say, a glacier journey up to a col and back.

By mixing these four factors (technical, non-technical, medium altitude and higher altitude) you will build up a sound base of experience without giving yourself a fright in the process.

On the Trient Glacier with the Aiguille du Chardonnet.

CLOTHING AND EQUIPMENT

It is a sad fact that the majority of British climbers visiting the Alps for the first time carry far too much.

EXAMPLE CHECKLIST

For a PD route with a glacier approach, mixed rock/snow and a night in a hut, the following is suitable:

Rucsack - Lightweight packs are essential. If you start with a big 70 litre pack, you will fill it with everything you think you might just need. So start with a 45 litre pack - it is big enough for the essentials.

Clothing - Clothing is a matter of personal choice, but something along the following lines is suitable:

thermal short-sleeved vest
cotton shirt + fleece
cotton trousers
Goretex-type jacket and over-trousers
sun hat + warm hat
finger gloves
gaiters (preferably not Super gaiters, which are too clumsy)
shorts for the walk to the hut (optional)

Odds and Ends

sun cream + lip salve
Insurance Certificate
sunglasses with side protection
camera + film
water bottle
money

TOP TIP: If in doubt, leave it out.

21

Climbing Equipment

harness + screwgate (alloy HMS)
long sling + screwgate (alloy HMS)
3 short prusiks
3 light alloy snaplinks
crampons + axe
1 ice screw
1 lightweight pulley

Group Equipment

small First Aid (plasters, Paracetamol)
map + compass
guidebook
group shelter
2 quick draws (using karabiners listed above)
rope (50m of UIAA single for a rope of 2 - 4)

Boots - For most Alpinism, leather boots are more suitable than plastic; as leather boots:
- are less sweaty for the feet.
- are more comfortable for the hut walks.
- are less clumsy to use on rock.
- if rigid soled, take crampons well.
- keep your socks drier than plastic, if you waterproof the boots regularly.

GENERAL POINTS

- without the rope, your pack should weigh no more than 17 - 23 lbs.
- as the grade increases, so does the amount of climbing gear you need. So, for an AD you might carry 4 or 5 Rocks (say 3,4,5,7 + 8), 5 quick draws, and a belay/abseil device.
- if you carry lots of safety equipment and spare this and spare that, all you will guarantee is eventually having to use it.

CREVASSE RESCUE

There are many methods of crevasse rescue, most of them fairly similar but with small variations or refinements. The number of people on the surface and the amount of rope available are the main factors in determining the method you use.

Except as part of a course, it is not the sort of thing the average climbing pair are likely to practise ("Hold on a minute while I jump into this crevasse. I want to see if I can remember what I read in that book...."). But it doesn't have to be as realistic as that. In a spare hour you can go through all the systems described here by pulling the car or a friend across the camp site. You do not need a vertical crag, because in reality most glaciers are nearer the horizontal than the vertical.

The following are well tested methods starting with the easiest. For simplicity the person in the crevasse is referred to as the casualty.

FRENCH PRUSIKS ARE USED THROUGHOUT AS THEY WORK IN ALL THESE SITUATIONS.

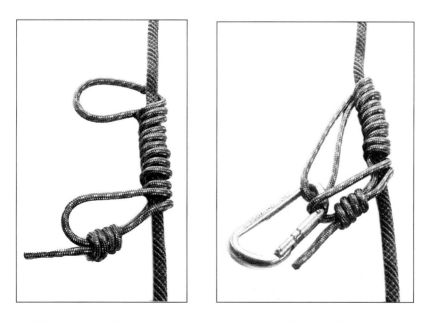

A 165CM LENGTH OF 6MM CORD WHEN TIED WITH A DOUBLE FISHERMAN'S MAKES A 60CM LOOP WHICH IS A USEFUL SIZE.

HOLDING THE FALL

But to start with, the fall must be held. An obvious point which is often over-looked. If you observe the following points, crevasse rescue almost becomes obsolete, because there won't be a problem in the first place.

- keep correct spacing (see 'Glacier Travel').

- stay alert and keep good rope management, however tired.

- when the person falls in, hit the snow with the axe in the self-arrest position.

- get your feet well dug-in.

- if you feel confident that you can hold the weight of the casualty, ask others to come forward to you; but as they come forward they should slide the rope through their French prusiks. If you start to slip, they can immediately help to check you.

1. CLIMB OUT

It may be that the edges of the crevasse are set back at an angle and the casualty can climb out. Or he may be able to walk along a bridge and get out at one end.

2. STRAIGHT HAUL

If there are enough of you on the surface (at least 5 people) it will probably be quickest and easiest to simply haul the casualty out.

Before hauling:

- check that the casualty is uninjured by going (roped of course) to the lip of the crevasse and making contact.
- if there is a snow lip to the edge of the crevasse, pad it with an ice axe or rucksack to prevent the rope cutting in.

Points

- The people hauling should stand still and take the rope in hand over hand, otherwise they might walk backwards into a crevasse.

3. ASSISTED HOIST

Anchor: make an anchor (see 'Snow/Ice Belays').

Tie-off the Rope:

- attach the anchor to your prusik.

- don't leave the casualty hanging off your prusik, but tie the rope off with a slippery hitch. To do this you will probably have to take off one coil.

- you can now escape from the system.

A SLIPPERY HITCH

Second Rope:

-TAKE A SECOND ROPE AND TIE ONE END OFF TO THE ANCHOR.

- DROP A LOOP OF THE SECOND ROPE TO THE CASUALTY, WITH A SCREWGATE AND PUL-LEY.

- TELL THE CASUALTY TO ATTACH THE SCREW-GATE TO THE MAIN BELAY LOOP OF HIS HARNESS OR TO THE ORIGINAL KNOT WITH WHICH HE TIED IN.

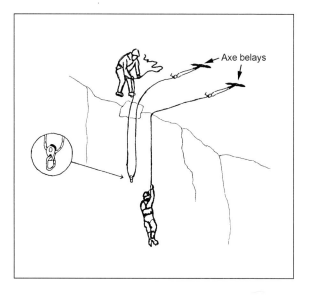

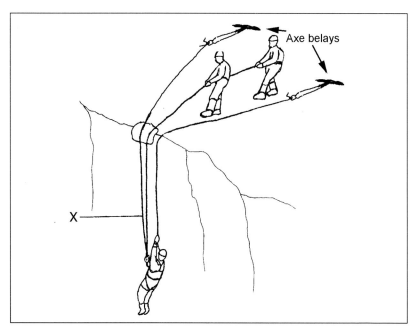

THE ASSISTED HOIST

Padding:

- pad the lip of the crevasse under the second rope with an ice axe or rucsack.

Hauling:

- as you haul, the casualty can help himself by pulling up on the fixed end (marked 'x' in the diagram).

- every now and then take in the original rope as a back-up.

Points:

- GETTING THE ANCHOR KRAB INTO YOUR PRUSIK IS EASIER IF YOU HAVE A SPARE SNAPLINK CLIPPED INTO YOUR PRUSIK - CLIP THIS INTO THE ANCHOR.

- you need enough rope to be able to get the loop down to the casualty.

- the casualty can help with the hauling.

- to make it easier on yourself, attach a prusik to the hauling rope and clip it to your harness. This means you can use the strength in your legs for hauling.

- by using a second rope which is padded at the lip, you avoid the problem of a casualty coming up under the lip.

4. PULLEY SYSTEM USING A SECOND ROPE

Anchor - as above.

Tie-off the Rope - as above.

Second Rope - drop a new end of rope with a screwgate, and tell the casualty to clip it in to his main belay loop.

Padding - as above

Pulley System:

- SET UP A PULLEY SYS-
TEM ON THE NEW ROPE,
USING A FRENCH
PRUSIK AS A CLUTCH
AND USING ANOTHER
PRUSIK + PULLEY FOR
HAULING.

- CHECK THAT THE
HAULING PRUSIK GRIPS
AND THAT THE CLUTCH
WORKS PROPERLY.

Hauling:

- as you haul, the hauling prusik will come up to the anchor. Ease off so that the clutch prusik engages; move the hauling prusik back down; and away you go again.

Points:

- if you don't have enough rope for the assisted hoist, this method at least allows you to pad under the rope you are going to haul on.

- take-in the original rope through its prusik as a back-up.

5. PULLEY SYSTEM ON THE ORIGINAL ROPE

Anchor and Tie-off - as above.

Padding - try to get padding under the original rope.

Pulley System - set up a pulley system on the original rope as above.

Hauling:

- before hauling, undo the slippery hitch.

- otherwise as above.

Undercut lips

If there is a bad lip to the crevasse the casualty may come up under it. If this happens, consider which is the best anchor: your little ice axe or your 6´ friend stuck under the lip? If you keep on hauling, the anchor might fail. Go to the lip and try to kick some of the snow away. Do make sure you are secured, and do not, on any account, use an ice axe as you might cut the loaded rope.

```
        Top Tip: buy a lightweight pulley.
```

6. PRUSIKING OUT

This is usually the method of choice when there are only two of you; one in the crevasse and one on the surface. It is vital that the fall is held; and once held, that it stays that way. The consequences of both going into the same crevasse are too awful to even consider.

Therefore it is better for the one on the surface to stay on the rope with their feet well dug in and axe in vertically, and not to try and set up an anchor when things might go wrong.

- the original prusik is your body prusik.

- put on a second prusik below this one . Clip a krab and sling to it, and adjust the sling with an overhand knot so that it fits one foot comfortably.

- move up the foot prusik, then stand up.

- move up the body prusik.

- continue to the top.

Points:

- it is easier to prusik up a weighted rope, so tie an overhand knot in below you and clip the rucksack in.

- just in case the prusiks start slipping, tie an occasional overhand knot in the rope below you.

- to have any chance of success, this must be practised. A tree is as good a place as any.

- if you have been travelling with overhand knots in the rope (see 'Glacier Travel') you cannot prusik up the rope. Instead, clip the overhand knots with slings and climb up - one short one for the body and one long one for the foot.

PRUSIKING OUT

**TOP TIP: avoid crevasse rescue in the first
place by roping-up and by staying alert.**

ETHICS

This is perhaps a rather pompous title for a short chapter covering one or two do's and don'ts.

PATHS/TRACKS

It is normal for those going up to have the right of way. So, if descending, it is polite to stand still and let them come past. If overtaking, keep well out of the way of the party you are overtaking. On a track up a glacier or snow slope, it is up to you, as the overtaking party, to step out of the track. Make sure your rope doesn't get under the feet of the party being overtaken.

HUTS

Leave your axe and crampons outside or in the porch area.

OVERTAKING ON ROUTES

If you catch up with a slower party on a route, ask politely if you can go past. In most cases this will be readily and friendly agreed to. But on the rare occasions where your request is ignored or refused, overtake anyway. If you do not overtake, you may fall badly behind guidebook time with the following results:

- a late descent in poor conditions (balling-up crampons, rockfall, weak crevasse bridges, electric storm).

- having to abandon the route and abseil off.

- an involuntary bivouac.

CALLS OF NATURE

If you get 'caught short', move away from paths and other areas where people congregate. Bury it under stones or in the snow.

AXES AND CRAMPONS

If you carry them unprotected on your rucsack they may injure someone. Crampons are best carried inside the sac, wrapped up in a crampon bag. The axe might fit well in the compression straps, spike down. On lifts and in buses etc. it might be best to carry your axe in your hand.

PULLING ON GEAR

On long Alpine routes speed is a vital factor and most Alpinists will have pulled on gear at some time or another. Some try to avoid doing so; others do it regularly. Few Alpinists have an ethical problem with it - not if it makes the difference between getting off and getting caught in a thunderstorm.

TOP TIP: light + light = heavy.

FIRST AID

The most likely things to go wrong are:

BLISTERS - Blisters can to an extent be prevented by strapping the feet up beforehand using a shiny zinc-oxide strapping - shiny does not stick to the socks. With two pairs of socks you are more likely to get blisters as the socks ruck up against each other forming pressure points. Try wearing just the one pair.

HEADACHES - Most of us get a headache at some time as we acclimatise. Immediate relief can be had from a couple of Asprin or Paracetamol.

BLEEDING - The treatment for bleeding, even serious bleeding, is direct pressure. A glove or your vest will do fine, but you may prefer to carry a wound dressing.

SPRAIN - A tightly wrapped crepe bandage might make a big difference to your ability to hobble down to the hut.

FIRST AID KIT

Aspirin or Paracetamol
zinc-oxide
some plaster
wound dressing (optional)
crepe bandage (optional)

If you go the other way and prepare for every eventuality, you will be carrying half a pharmacy around the mountain. It is unlikely you will ever need it; and you can improvise using your clothes and what you have in your rucsack. A large First Aid Kit cuts across the overriding need to travel light.

> **TOP TIP: First Aid is exactly that - not paramedic casualty treatment.**

FOOTWORK

In Britain we usually walk on easy ground to the foot of the crag, get the ropes out and do the climb, and then walk off down an easy path.

In the Alps, on the other hand, we spend a lot of time on easy ground but with a dreadful penalty for tripping over. Some of the paths up to the huts have enormous drops off to the side. Easy angled glaciers can steepen quickly to become steep snow or ice. And many routes (whether rock, snow, ice or a mixture) have easy sections mixed in with the harder technical pitches.

So, in the Alps, it is especially important to develop good footwork.

CRAMPONS

Look at your crampons and see how many points are designed for forward grip and how many for sideways.

When putting them on, have any buckles on the outside, and tuck loose straps away.

It is easy to catch the front points in the strap of the other crampon (or in the gaiter or trouser leg) so avoid this potential trip by keeping the feet slightly apart and by angling the toes out - better to catch the heels than the front points.

Use all the bottom points whenever possible - usually 8.8 points are safer than 4, so angle your foot accordingly and avoid edging.

Keep front-pointing to a minimum, unless you enjoy pain and want to develop massive calf muscles. But when front-pointing, make sure you have all 4 points in by keeping the sole of your foot horizontal. If you raise your heels, only 2 points will be on - and 4 are better than 2.

On easy-angled slopes, it is easy enough to walk straight up the slope. But as it steepens, you may find that the calf muscles come under stress, and that this stress is relieved if you turn the feet slightly sideways. The steeper the slope gets, the more you should turn your feet sideways - until they are pointing slightly down the slope.

On mixed routes it is quite normal to keep the crampons on for short rock sections. It just depends whether you will save time by taking them off and then putting them on again. So practise climbing rock with your crampons - quite scary to start with, but you will soon find how effective they are.

WITHOUT CRAMPONS

On Ice and Snow - As the summer warms up, so the snow melts on the glaciers leaving bare ice. The typical situation is bare ice lower down, changing to snow-covered ice as you gain height. It is well worthwhile developing your ability to walk around on this bare ice without crampons, using the gritty bits for grip. The snow is likely to be better without crampons and you will save a lot of time if you can avoid having to continually change them. What happens in reality is that most people put their crampons on for the ice and keep them on for the snow - but wearing them for the snow is probably more tiring and they would be better off without them.

On Rock - Loose rock needs a gentle touch. Move as lightly as possible on your feet and avoid looking for handholds - they won't be any good.

STRESS-FREE WALKING

While your footwork must be safe, it is also worthwhile trying to develop a relaxed way of walking. Many Alpine days last 10 hours or more, so go light on your feet and try to reduce the stress on a particular muscle group by altering your style - i.e. alternate walking straight up with zig-zagging; alternate front-pointing with flat-footing.

"Look well to each step", Edward Whymper.

GLACIER TRAVEL

GLACIER FORMATION

A glacier is formed by the accumulation of snow in the high altitude permanent snowfields known as névé. The snow changes form; then it is compacted through the weight of further snowfalls; and it gradually turns to ice. As the glacier flows downhill like a river of ice, it continues to be fed from above by winter snowfalls and it comes to an end at the snout where the ice is melted.

Advancing or Retreating - A glacier is advancing when the snout is moving downhill, and it is retreating when the snout is moving back uphill. It depends on the balance between the feeding and the melting.

The Trient glacier in Switzerland has been advancing and retreating as follows:

Before 1800	no data available.
1800-1850	advanced a long way.
1850-1878	retreated 800m.
1878-1896	advanced 211m.
1896-1914	retreated 235m.
1915	back to where it was in 1878.
1915-1924	advanced 151m.
1925-1941	retreated 227m.
1942	advanced 3m.
1943-1952	retreated 315m.
1953-1957	no change.
1958-1960	advanced 40m.
1961	retreated 26m.
1962-1987	advanced 378m.
1988-1993	retreated 62m.

Since 1915 the overall change is an advance of 18m.

CREVASSES

The centre of the glacier flows quicker than the sides, and the surface flows quicker than the bottom. These differences in rate of flow create tension and crevasses form at right angles to the tension.

TYPES OF CREVASSES

The main types are:

Transverse - which run ACROSS the main flow of the glacier. The main places for these are:

- where the glacier steepens.

- on the outside of bends.

- where the glacier is squeezed.

Longitudinal - which run DOWN the flow. The main places for these are:

- where the glacier widens e.g. at the snout.

- where any part of it is raised in a longitudinal ridge by pressure of rock beneath.

Bergschrund or Rimaye - the big crevasse between the glacier and the permanent snowfield. Later in the season when the bridges have collapsed they may be impossible to cross. In descent it is often necessary to abseil over them, using a snow bollard as the anchor point.

Randkluft - the big crevasse between the glacier and the rock walls. Usually called the bergschrund, but at the risk of being pedantic, it should really be called a randkluft.

Crevasse Identification - A vital skill in safe glacier travel is the ability to identify where crevasses might be, and to decide whether they are transverse or longitudinal. The surface of the glacier gives some indication as to areas of tension. Not only can we see the surface of the glacier, but the map shows it with contour lines. Another big factor is the presence of rock ridges under the ice and we cannot see these - nor does the map help, except in showing those ridges which are visible.

Although it is possible to be fairly certain about some crevasses, much of the time it is guesswork.

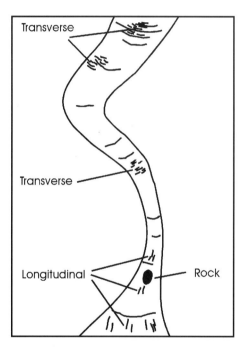

LIKELY PLACES FOR CREVASSES

Crevasse Bridges - In the heavy winter snow falls, some crevasses are filled in or bridged over. Then, in the early spring with the hot weather, some of this snow falls into the crevasses. But not all of it falls in, and so we are left with crevasses which are open in places and which are bridged over in others. At this stage, i.e. early spring, these bridges are very unreliable. As the year progresses into summer, the continuous processes of thaw and freeze result in bridges which are well-defined and strong. In summer, if you cross these bridges early in the morning or at any other time when the temperature is low, you will usually cross safely.

ROUTE FINDING ON A GLACIER

The safest line is the line of least resistance, avoiding:

- areas of steepness.
- known rock ridges.
- the outside of bends.

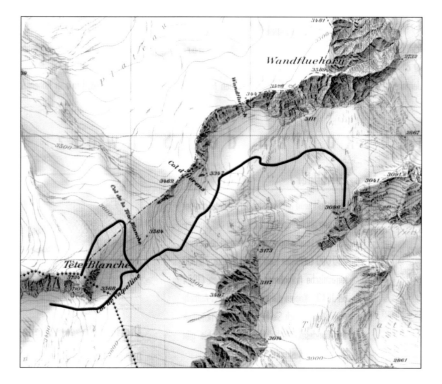

Map reproduced by permission of the Swiss Federal Office of Topography, 17.12.1997.

Safe line on a glacier

ICE-FALLS - are caused by a change in the gradient of the glacier resulting in a complicated jumble of ice with a mixture of longitudinal and transverse crevasses.

SERACS - are big unstable towers of ice. They occur in ice-falls and can fall over at any time as the main influence on them is gravity.

DRY AND WET GLACIERS

Dry Glaciers

A dry glacier is bare ice. The ice is often grey in colour due to the grit, dirt and stones in the surface. Any crevasses are clear to see, and it is therefore, normal to cross these glaciers without a rope.

If the angle is not steep and there is plenty of grit and stones, it may be easier to go without crampons. If in doubt wear crampons.

Sometimes it is necessary to walk parallel with the crevasses as you look for a way through, so safe footwork is essential.

As the day warms up, surface water increases. This can be to such an extent that actual rivers of water flow down the surface of the glacier, sometimes proving difficult to cross.

Wet Glaciers

A wet glacier is one covered with snow. The crevasses may be visible, or they may be hidden by the snow. As there is no way of telling whether there are hidden crevasses or not, it is essential to wear a rope. If the snow is not frozen hard, it will probably be easier to go without crampons.

As the day warms up, the bridges become weaker. A bridge which supported you at 04.00 in the morning might fail at midday.

Many people use totally inappropriate rope systems for glacier travel, systems which would simply not stand the test of someone falling in. Others have none at all.

However good you are, however experienced you are, the following facts are beyond discussion:

- there are crevasses in unexpected places.

- there are crevasses which are completely hidden.

- crevasses vary in depth from a few feet to hundreds of feet.

- crevasses vary in width from a few inches to over 45 ft/15 metres.

- bridges vary in depth from a few inches to several feet.

- bridges vary in strength.

Tracks on Glaciers - All that a track means is that someone went this way before. We don't know if they got there. So tracks, while obviously good to follow, do not by any means offer security, as hidden below them will be all sorts of holes and horror shows.

Undercut Lips - Crevasses sometimes have undercut lips of snow especially early in the season. They can collapse a surprisingly long way back from the edge in the same way as cornices collapse.

Cross Crevasses at a Right-angle

By crossing at a right-angle you reduce the risk of everyone falling into the same crevasse. If the crevasses are running parallel to your route, it is a good idea to offset the rope.

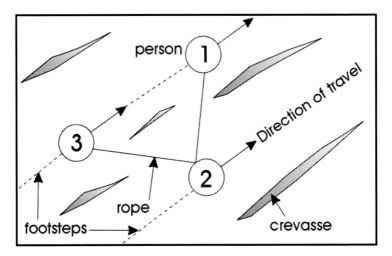

OFFSETTING THE ROPE

TAKING COILS

The centre of mass of your body is around your tummy button - i.e. above the suspension point of a sit harness. With a rucsack the centre of mass is moved up to the base of the sternum. If you fall into a crevasse there is a risk of inverting.

One solution is to wear a full-body harness which has a suspension point around the base of sternum - i.e. the same as the centre of mass. They are very suitable for glacier travel, but if you are going onto steep ground where there is a risk of a leader fall, they can result in severe back injury.

The answer is to wear a normal sit harness and to take body coils while on a glacier, in such a way that they lock off at the base of sternum. And then when climbing, use the sit harness on its own.

Method of taking coils:

(I) TAKE COILS OVER
THE SHOULDER AND
UNDER THE ARM, TEN-
SIONING EACH SO THAT
THEY ARE COMFORT-
ABLE. IF THEY ARE TOO
SLACK THEY WILL NOT
LOCK OFF CORRECTLY

(II) BRING A LOOP BACK
ROUND THE COILS

(III) TIE THIS LOOP IN AN OVERHAND KNOT ROUND THE LIVE ROPE MAKING SURE THAT THE NEW LOOP CREATED BY THE OVERHAND KNOT IS NO LONGER THAN 4'. IF IT IS LONGER, THE COILS WILL NOT LOCK OFF PROPERLY AT THE BASE OF STERNUM:

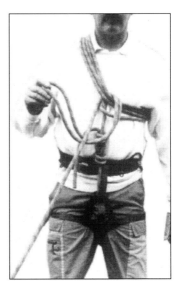

(IV) CLIP THE NEW LOOP INTO A SCREWGATE ON YOUR HARNESS.

IF YOU NOW FALL INTO A CREVASSE, THE ROPE LOCKS OFF ON THE COILS LEVEL WITH THE BASE OF STERNUM - A COMFORTABLE POSITION WITH NO RISK OF INVERTING.

PRUSIK: ROPE TO HARNESS

So far this system has resolved the case if you fall into a crevasse. But if your friend falls in and you have to hold the fall, the pull comes high on you level with the sternum and this is harder to hold than if the pull comes from low down.

THE ANSWER IS TO ATTACH A FRENCH PRUSIK TO THE ROPE AND TO CLIP THIS TO YOUR HARNESS WITH A SNAPLINK.

IF YOU FALL IN, PULL THE PRUSIK DOWN AND THE SUSPENSION POINT COMES BACK TO THE BASE OF STERNUM.

SPACINGS

First, measure your rope to see how many arm spans there are. An arm span is about the same as a body coil. For the following examples, I am assuming 30 body coils for a 50m. rope; and I allow one coil per person for tying-in.

The recommended spacings between each person are recommendations for average conditions. As you gain experience you will find there are occasions when it is better to either reduce or to lengthen them.

People in the middle of the rope take two coils for tying-off in order to raise the suspension point.

Two people on the rope

Spacing between each person: 12 coils

30 coils less 2 for tying-in   28
Recommended spacing   <u>12</u>

Available for body coils   16

So each person takes 8 body coils

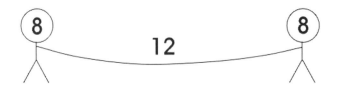

Three people on the rope

Spacing between each person: 6 coils.

30 coils less 3 for tying-in	27
Recommended spacing 6 x 2	<u>12</u>
Available for body coils	15
Middle person	<u>2</u>
	<u>13</u>

One end person takes 7, the other takes 6.

Four people on the rope

Spacing between each person: 5 coils.

30 coils less 4 for tying-in	26
Recommended spacing 5 x 3	<u>15</u>
Available for body coils	11
Middle people: 2 x 2	<u>4</u>
	<u>7</u>

One end person takes 4, the other takes 3.

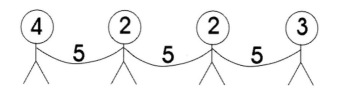

KNOTTED ROPE

When there are just two people on the rope, the big danger is that one person falls into a crevasse and the other person gets pulled in after him. This is particularly so when there is an imbalance in body weight and the heavier person goes in.

The priority is for the lighter person to be able to hold the fall. This can be helped by tying overhand knots in the rope.

It is a highly recommended practice whenever there are two on the rope and the crevasses are at all suspect.

Method:

- tie about 20 overhand knots in front of each person.

- the gap between each knot should be 8"-9".

- pull each knot tight as you make it, otherwise they tighten up when the person goes in and he will drop further than necessary.

- this leaves a spacing of 12 coils: 3 with knots in front of each person and 6 without knots in the middle.

- there will not be enough rope for you to have body coils, but the holding of the fall is more important than the suspension issue.

Holding the fall - When the person falls in, hit the ground as normal and get dug in. You will be pleasantly surprised how easy it is to hold the casualty's weight, because the knots will have dug in to the lip of the crevasse.

Rescue - The casualty climbs up the knotted rope, clipping karabiners with slings into the overhand knots - one short for his body and one long for a foot.

TYPE OF ROPE - For glacier travel a UIAA half-rope is enough. If you are going to climb, you will either have two half-ropes, or a UIAA single. You can safely do the glacier part using just one of the half-ropes.

ROPE MANAGEMENT - There are two ways of having the rope.

Normal - The rope just touches the ground and goes up to the person in front. There is no slack.

Tight - If the person in front is worried about crevasses he asks for a tight rope, and this means hawser tight between each person. To get a tight rope quickly, either step back a few paces or take the rope in through your prusik.

Handcoils - should never be carried. It just means that you will fall that extra distance and probably catapult the next person in after you.

Zig-zagging - On steeper ground it may be necessary to zig-zag. As you turn each corner, there is a conflict of interests between:

- avoiding slack in the rope.
- keeping a steady pace going.

It is a compromise. If the crevasses are not bad and it is frozen, keep the steady pace going and allow the slack to accumulate. But if you are concerned about the crevasses, either keep the rope fairly tight or alter course and go straight up the slope - so avoiding the issue by crossing the transverse crevasses at a right angle.

TOP TIP: Always rope-up on a snow-covered glacier, whatever anyone else does. You will be right and they will be wrong.

GRADINGS

A word of caution: do not go too far in trying to equate your British grade to an Alpine one. And the higher the altitude, the less you should do it. A French V+ on a roadside crag might feel like a 4c back home, but on a long route at altitude it is a very different affair. Altitude, tiredness, the need to get a move on, maybe climbing in big boots - all combine to make it feel a lot harder.

TECHNICAL GRADING

UIAA	UK	France	
III	V Diff	III	
IV−		IV−	
IV	M Severe	IV	
IV+	4a	IV+	
V−		V−	
V	4b	V	
V+			5a
VI−	4c	V+	5b
VI	5a		5c
VI+	5b	6a	
VII−			
VII	5c	6b	
VII+	6a	6c	
VIII−			
VIII	6b	7a	
VIII+		7b	
IX−			
IX	6c	7c	
IX+			

ADJECTIVAL GRADINGS

These take into account:

- the general level of technical difficulty.

- the seriousness of the route (i.e. length, altitude, danger from rockfall etc, commitment).

FRENCH	**GERMAN**
F Facile	L Leicht
PD Peu Difficile	WS Wenig Schwierig
AD Assez Difficile	ZS Ziemlich Schwierig
D Difficile	S Schwierig
TD Trés Difficile	SS Sehr Schwierig
ED Extrêment Difficile	AS Ausserst Schwierig

Each grade is further subdivided into (–) and (+).

There seems no point in translating them into English. For example, you could translate AD into Fairly Difficult and yet that is harder than British Difficult. And then D into Difficult, and that is harder still....

As you gain experience you will learn what to expect to find on them. For example:

F   Steep walking routes, rock scrambling, easy snow slopes, glaciers with some crevasses.

F+   Sustained rock scrambling, crevassed glaciers.

PD- Rock climbing with short pitches of II, steep snow slopes to 45°, heavily crevassed glaciers.

PD Rock climbing with short pitches of II and III, steep snow/ice slopes to 50°, difficult glaciers, narrow ridges.

PD+ Sustained rock climbing with pitches III and III+, steep snow + ice slopes.

AD- Short rock pitches of III+ and IV-, short snow/ice faces.

AD Fairly difficult and serious climbs with pitches of III and IV, long snow/ice faces at 50° plus.

AD+ More sustained AD's with delicate pitches of III and IV,complex snow/ice.

D- Hard rock climbing to IV+ and V-, ice pitches of Scottish 3.

D Sustained rock at IV+ and V, sustained snow/ice of 55°.

D+ More technical pitches at V- and V.

TD- Committing routes often with bivouac, rock pitches of V and sustained snow/ice 55°-60°.

TD Very difficult technical climbing with pitches of V and V+.

ED Extremely serious climbs with long sustained difficulties.

GUIDEBOOK TIME

Most guidebooks have a recommended time for the route which is based on a reasonably competent party with the route in good condition. The problem for British climbers coming to the Alps for the first time is that the time is estimated with local climbers (e.g. French) in mind and:

- they are generally very good.

- they carry very little, relying on speed and judgement.

- they are acclimatised, fit, and accustomed to such things as crevasses.

- they use rope techniques which appear to the novice British climber to be dangerous, but which are actually effective and fast.

So what is the hurry ? Well, it is not a hurry, rather an unhurried but fast and fluent performance. The reason is that Alpine routes are long and many have quite difficult descents and it is important to complete difficult sections of the descent while the conditions are still good. In broad terms you aim to be on the summit between 08.00 - 09.00.

Consider this hypothetical descent from a summit of 3,800m with the following two situations:

i)   crampon down snow, aspect NW.

ii)   move round to the S to crampon down snow, aspect SE.

iii)   abseil down a steep snow couloir for 4 pitches, aspect S.

iv)   crampon down the rest of the snow couloir.

v)   a glacier descent to the hut with a bergschrund and several crevasses.

Situation (A)

If you are at the summit at 08.00, the snow at the top will be frozen and good to descend on crampons (say 1/2hr.); it is now 09.30-10.00 and the rest of the couloir should be reasonable on crampons. The bridge over the bergschrund will still be frozen, and the rest of the crevasse bridges should not be too bad. You get back to the hut by 11.30-12.00 hrs.

Situation (B)

But what about the party which arrives at the summit at 11.00 hrs? The snow facing NW will still be frozen - no problem. But the snow facing SE will be soft from the sun, so your crampons will ball up. You move more slowly as you clear your crampons, and there is a real risk of a fall. The abseil pitches are started at, say, 12.00 hrs. when there is a risk of rockfall from the rocks which have been loosened by the sun. The rest of the couloir is descended with a rockfall risk and balling-up crampons, and the bridge over the bergschrund is dripping with water. Suddenly it isn't much fun any more - and you still have a crevassed glacier to descend - with unfrozen bridges. If you are lucky you get back to the hut at 17.00-18.00 hrs.

There are of course times when it is perfectly reasonable to go over the guidebook time. If you arrive at the top and the conditions will definitely stay good for the descent, there is nothing better than sitting up there for an hour or so enjoying the view.

But the general rule is: move at guidebook time.

There are many factors involved, some covered in separate chapters.

PREPARATION

Sort your rucsack the day before so everything is ready and you know where individual items are.

Check the map and route description. And if unfamiliar with the route, go out during the previous afternoon and have a look at the first hour or so - it is very frustrating to get lost on easy ground in the dark.

GO LIGHT

Carry the minimum - (See 'Clothing and Equipment').

Remember: safety is not brought in by buying every piece of safety equipment. Safety lies in good personal skills combined with sound judgment.

EARLY START

Get up in time and aim to leave the hut within 45min - time to linger over breakfast some other time.

ALPINE PACE

Develop the steady pace of Alpinists. It is not fast, but it is steady and unrelenting. Try to keep stops to a minimum, because every time you stop it is bound to take longer than planned - the stop for a drink results in the sun cream going on, the fleece off, a quick photograph....

MOVING TOGETHER

The ability to move together safely and fluently is potentially the biggest time saver. (See Chapter 'Moving Together').

LEADING + SECONDING

In Britain partners of equal ability will usually alternate leads. In the Alps it is often better for one person to lead all the route, or at least half and to then change round. The reason for this is that the leader can get into 'leader' mode - i.e. finding the route and not falling off. The second gets into 'seconding' mode which is going as fast as possible, maybe pulling on some of the gear (see 'Ethics'). To change over at every stance is disruptive and slows things up.

As a general rule, allow 20min per pitch: 15min to lead it and 5min to second it.

PROGRESSION

If you lead, say, VS 4c at home you might look at the gradings and see this equates to French V+ and chose a TD route as your first route. If you do (and you won't be the first) you will be in for something of a shock. More suitable would be a PD/PD-, and at modest altitude. If that goes will, either put the grade up or the altitude - but not both at the same time.

Build up your speed on the easy routes. They are worthwhile in their own right and you will find there is a lot to learn.

The harder routes will always be there; but if you go for them too soon, you might not.

TOP TIP: go at guidebook time.

HUTS

Most huts belong to the Alpine club of the country, although in Austria many of the huts are German Alpine Club. There are also private huts, some belonging to the local Guides' Association - and these are usually a little more expensive. The Austrian huts are the best.

BOOKING

Always book in advance. If you cannot speak the language, ask the local Tourist Office for help - and they will have a list of numbers. When booking the guardian will probably ask you if you are going to take meals.

RECIPROCAL RIGHTS

By being a member of one of the Alpine clubs you get a reduction on the overnight charge, but not on the meals. And this applies to whichever country you are in. If you are a member of the British Mountaineering Council you need to get a Reciprocal Rights card in addition to the Membership Card.

Membership often includes insurance.

Currently, it is worth getting this reciprocal arrangement if you are going to spend 5 or more nights in huts during the year.

FACILITIES

The food varies enormously from a set meal of adequate proportions but simple fare, to restaurant type service with waitresses in many Austrian huts. Vegetarians are not usually well catered for - the meat being replaced with a slab of cheese or an omelette.

The beds are usually mattresses with two blankets and a pillow, often with 30 or more people to a dormitory. Some huts have smaller rooms, and many Austrian huts have rooms with beds and sheets. Ear plugs can help you get a reasonable night's sleep.

Toilets are often basic although an increasing number of huts are being modified to include indoor toilets with running water. As many huts have very limited water supplies, the outside thunderbox is likely to be part of the Alpine scene for many years to come.

CHECKING-IN

When you arrive, go and see the guardian who will check your name against the bookings, probably ask for your Alpine Club card, tell you where your bed is and the time of the evening meal.

But before you go and see the guardian, leave your axe and crampons outside and change your boots for a pair of the hut slippers which are supplied.

BEDROOMS

Bedrooms are for sleeping, an obvious point which is frequently over-looked. People may be resting or sleeping at any time of the day, so do please respect that. Rucsacks should should be sorted elsewhere - rustling polybags are particularly disturbing. And in some huts rucsacks are not allowed in the bedrooms, for this reason.

In the morning blankets should be neatly folded.

PAYMENT - is usually by cash, local Bank cheques or Eurocheques. Do not rely on credit or charge cards being accepted.

THE GUARDIAN

Guardians work long hours with little privacy. They will supply all main meals, plus drinks and snacks through the day. But they also need time to eat and have time off, so please respect that and if necessary come back later.

SELF-COOKING

French Alpine Club huts have rooms where you can cook your own food. There is usually a supply of water, but little else; so you should take your own stove etc. In Swiss huts this is not allowed, but they will cook your food for you. However, if you take your won food you should bear in mind that the guardian makes his living from the supply of food and drink, so you can hardly expect to be his favourite customer.

Looking down on a bergschrund

LIGHTNING

It is every Alpinist's worst nightmare to be caught in an electric storm. They can come in so quickly and with such ferocity that you may have nowhere to go.

Avoid them at all costs. The chapter 'Weather' describes the systems to watch for. Change your plans to a lower and shorter route which you can complete comfortably in time.

The cloud is the cumulonimbus and as it grows, so the water droplets inside it are hurled up and down. If they freeze they shatter; and as they shatter there is a separation of electrical charges - the positive charges attach to the ice crystals and the negative charges attach to the hail. A discharge (lightning) takes place, coupled with an explosive expansion of air (thunder). The lightning hits the ground when the discharge takes place between the negatively charged hail and positively charged ground.

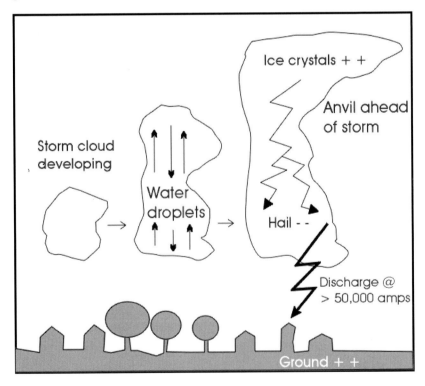

WARNING SIGNS

The two systems which cause thunderstorms are (a) cold fronts and (b) hot weather. The best warning of (a) is the weather chart showing a cold front, with an immediate warning of a noticeable drop in pressure. The best warning of (b) is the weather chart showing a weak pressure gradient, with immediate warnings of the weather feeling heavy and the build up of *altocumulus castellanus* or *altocumulus flocus.*

The French word for thunderstorms is 'orages'.

If you are on a summit or exposed ridge you may hear crackling sounds and your ice axe may hum or spark. Your hair may stand on end and may even glow with a bluish light (the St. Elmo's Fire).

GETTING OFF THE MOUNTAIN

But unfortunately the time will come when you do get caught, because every Alpinist gets caught sooner or later. Make every effort to get off the mountain. If you haven't been running for some time, now is the time to take it up again.

If you are on an exposed ridge, try to get along it and down the easy slopes back to the hut. But if that isn't going to work, it will probably be best to abseil off the ridge. Ideally pick a place where you can leave the abseil ropes in place and move off to one side.

THE POSITION

SIT OUT IN THE OPEN
ON YOUR RUCKSACK,
HEELS ONLY ON THE
GROUND, HEAD DOWN
BETWEEN YOUR ARMS.

Lightning

A group bivvy shelter is good because it will not only help you stay dry, but you can share the horror of the moment with your friends.

PLACES TO AVOID

- ridges, as you are particularly exposed to bolt lightning coming in at you horizontally.

- under boulders and in the entrance to caves as the lightning is looking for the shortest way to earth and you might provide the link.

- in the line of cracks in the rock, because the lightning may follow the crack down.

METAL OBJECTS

Put your axe, crampons and other climbing hardware at least 20 metres away from you, as the lightning will be attracted to them.

TREES

If you are down below the tree-line avoid the temptation of sheltering underneath a big tree, because it is the most likely object around to be hit.

IF STRUCK

Not all lightning strikes are fatal. But if someone is struck and they stop breathing, start rescucitation straight away. The strike might have caused other problems, e.g. loss of gloves, so have a good check round.

TOP TIP: develop a healthy terror of thunderstorms.

MOVING TOGETHER

Your first sight of two Continental climbers rattling past you, joined together by a few feet of rope, will come as a bit of a shock. What looks very dangerous is compounded by the minuscule size of their rucsacks.

The truth is: they have got it right and you haven't .....yet.

Moving together is an essential skill for every Alpine route. It is the only way of getting up and down these big routes in time.

SNOW

The presumption in guidebook times is that climbers will move together on the equivalent of Scottish Grade 1. If you cannot solo that grade of ground, you cannot safely move together on it - and so you should go away and practise, and come back another day.

It is the equivalent to soloing, except worse: if one of you comes off, the other is off as well. So why do it?

- for a start, you will probably have had the rope on for the glacier. It is quicker to throw on a few coils than to take the rope off and put it away in the rucsack.

- in any case, you will probably need the rope again later for the rock pitches, or for the descent.

- and it may be that the steep snow gets a bit icy and difficult. Perhaps one of you runs out of bottle. It is then easy to take off the coils and take a belay. Compare that with dancing about on your front points trying to get the rope out of your rucsack - if you were frightened before, you'll be terrified now.

Levels on snow - it is perhaps useful to think of the following different grades of difficulty and their respective rope techniques.

LEVEL 1 - moving together as close as possible, say 3 metres apart, with the rope going down between the leader's legs and fairly tight between you. If the second slips, the leader may hold him. The leader must not slip.

LEVEL 2 - once Level 1 becomes unsuitable, it is best to run the rope right out and take belays, either direct or indirect - see below.

ROCK

Most routes have sections at the technical grade interspersed with easier sections of scrambling where you can move together.

Levels on rock

LEVEL 1 - easy scrambling ground where you move together a few feet apart with about 5 body coils held in your hands as hand coils.

LEVEL 2 - more exposed and slightly harder ground where you run the 5 body coils out between you, so that you move together but spread out. The leader drops the rope in behind spikes of rock. If necessary he puts on a sling, clips a peg or slots in a nut. The objective is that both of you keep moving at the same time.

LEVEL 3 - the leader does a move which he thinks might be hard for the second, so he puts the rope round a spike and brings the second up. The selection of sound spikes is vital.

LEVEL 4 - the pitch looks hard and is longer than the 5 body coils you have out. The leader takes off the necessary additional coils from round his body. As he leads on up, the second pays out the rope through his gloved hands and the leader slots in runners as necessary. The leader must be confident to do this one.

LEVEL 5 - harder again, enough to make the leader stop and think. The second puts on an anchor and belays the leader - either a body belay or using a belay device. The leader leads on up, placing runners as necessary, and brings the second up on a direct belay.

LEVEL 6 - the normal one you are used to back in Britain, with both the second and the leader tied off onto anchors and belaying indirectly.

POINTS:

- be alert to the changing terrain and continually change from one technique to the other.

- safety must be paramount, but remember that speed is safety so try to get back to Level 1 or 2 whenever possible.

- moving together needs practice; but when you get good at it, it is incredibly effective.

DIRECT BELAYS

A direct belay may be:

- a rock spike: you place the rope round the spike and take it in as the second climbs. You are relying on the friction of the rope round the rock. Test that the spike is sound by thumping it with your gloved hand (a hollow sound indicates looseness). Give it a careful pull.

- a peg or bolt in place. Clip it with a screwgate, preferably an HMS, and use an Italian Friction Hitch. In-situ pegs and bolts can usually be relied on, but always have a close look at them and give them a tug.

**TOP TIP: it is moving together
and not standing together**

Moving Together on Rock, Level 1.

NAVIGATION

DIFFERENCES BETWEEN MAPS

Shading - If you open a Swiss map (Carte Nationale de la Suisse) or an Austrian map (Alpenvereinskarte), you will probably be impressed by the three dimensional effect. The map is almost a photograph with ridges and glaciers very obvious. Much of this is due to shading. For example, the Swiss maps have the slopes facing north and west shaded lighter than those facing south and east.

Grid Lines - French maps have very few; Austrian maps none at all. This means that taking off compass bearings is slightly more haphazard, and you cannot give grid references.

Magnetic Variation - This is much less than in Britain and for practical purposes is ignored.

Ski Routes - The ski routes are marked on some maps and are recommended routes for winter and spring tourers. On the back of some maps (e.g. the Swiss 1:50,000 and the Austrian 1:25,000) are short route descriptions in guidebook form, giving approximate times. These ski routes may coincide with the summer route, but not necessarily.

ACCURACY OF GLACIER INFORMATION

If the balance between feeding and melting is equal, the glacier keeps its shape. If the balance is unequal, the glacier will be either advancing or retreating. In the Alps, some are advancing, some retreating and some are stable; and if the survey was last done several years ago, the information on the map may be inaccurate.

For example:

- the snout may be a long way further back than indicated on the map, easily as much as 200 vertical metres or one kilometre horizontally.

- a guidebook may advise a summer route which goes up the glacier for a while and then takes to the rocks at the side. If the glacier has retreated, the rocks which have subsequently been exposed may be extremely smooth and unclimbable; and your 'easy glacier route' starts to take on different dimensions.

- a hut which was once built by the side of the glacier may now be left perched well above it. For example, the Konkordia Hut in the Bernese Oberland has a long section of ladder leading up to it.

- crevasses which are marked on the map may not be there; and more important, a glacier which is marked as being crevasse free may become heavily crevassed.

NAVIGATION SKILLS

Map Reading - Most navigation is done by map reading as the weather is usually good enough to see and identify features. If the weather is not good enough for that you probably will not have set off in the first place because of the length of the routes and of the problems of negotiating crevassed glaciers in bad weather.

Compass - A compass is useful for identifying features, and is essential for following a bearing in poor visibility. Many Alpine routes require a start in the darkness of night, and it may be that a compass bearing is needed - but not that often, as popular routes are usually marked with paths, cairns and tracks on the glaciers; and the skill is in picking these up. If you are in doubt about the section you will have to do in the dark, you should arrive at the hut in good time on the day before, giving yourself the time to go and have a look at this section in the daylight.

Altimeters - Altimeters are very useful in the Alps, where you are often on a definite feature (like a long ridge or glacier), and where the problem is knowing how far along the feature you are. Altimeters are therefore particularly useful in the following situations:

(i) RIDGES - If you are going up or down a will-defined ridge, a compass bearing is unnecessary if you keep to the crest of the ridge. But it can be difficult to tell in bad visibility how far along the ridge you have gone. An accurate estimate of time will help, but an altimeter is more accurate and very simple to use.

(ii) GLACIERS - It helps you avoid crevassed areas which are marked on the map.

TYPES OF ALTIMETER - The Thommen altimeter is the best, although expensive. It is small, easy to read, very reliable and strongly made. Each calibration is ten metres and it is possible to be accurate to this degree. Others like the Casio and Avocet combine an altimeter with a watch, giving you multi-functions at a reasonable price.

METHOD OF USE - Full instructions come with the instrument, but the following points are worth noting.

- since it works off barometric pressure the altimeter is affected by changes in the weather. It must be continually adjusted by resetting it at known points. If you know, for example, that a trough of low pressure is coming through, be careful about this point.

- for the same reason, if you go for more than 10 kilometres horizontal distance or for more than 500 vertical metres without resetting it, it may be inaccurate.

- the speed at which you travel is important. If you are moving slowly, it could take 2 hours to cover 5 kilometres: and 2 hours is more than enough for pressure to change and for the instrument to be inaccurate.

- the altimeter is affected by temperature changes. There is a complicated procedure for correcting this, but provided you reset regularly on known points, this can be (and in practice invariably is) ignored.

- in the hut you can use it overnight as a barometer. Either set it to zero or to the height of the hut. If in the morning the instrument shows the height of the hut to be higher than it actually is, the pressure has dropped. If it shows the height to be lower, the pressure has risen.

- some cheaper altimeters have calibrations every 50 metres or more. These are useless for mountain navigation, as the interval between calibrations is too great. A 10 metre interval is recommended.

Aspect of Slope

THE ASPECT OF A PARTICULAR SLOPE IS THE DIRECTION IT FACES. IN THE EXAMPLE, THE SLOPE AB HAS AN ASPECT OF C. 330°.

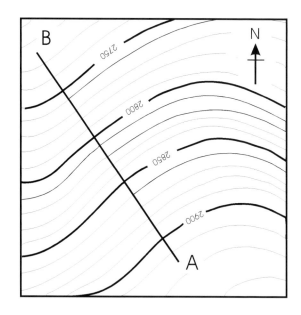

Imagine you have been out for some time in really bad visibility, and that you are descending a slope which has dangerous outcrops on it. Suppose you are not sure where you are on the slope, and you want to be sure you are not going to walk over the outcrops. All you can see is the slope you are on, and you can't even see much of that. Take the aspect of the slope by:

- POINT THE COMPASS DOWN THE SLOPE AND READ THE BEARING. CONVERT TO GRID.

- PUT THE COMPASS ON THE MAP. KEEPING THE ORIENTING LINES IN THE COMPASS BASE PARALLEL WITH THE GRID LINES ON THE MAP, AND KEEPING THE ORIENTING ARROW NORTH ON THE MAP, SLIDE THE COMPASS ALONG YOUR PRESUMED ROUTE.

- WATCH THE LONG SIDE OF THE COMPASS. WHEN IT CROSSES THE CONTOUR LINES AT RIGHT ANGLES, THIS IS THE SLOPE YOU ARE ON.

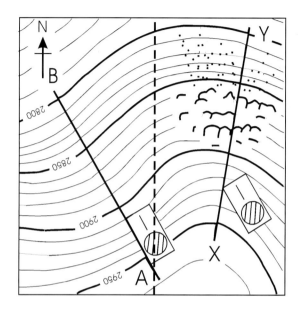

YOU ARE ON AB AND NOT XY.

Aspect of The Slope does not tell you where you are: it tells you that you are on a slope of a certain aspect. When combined with map reading and especially with an altimeter, you should know exactly where you are.

TOP TIP: buy an altimeter.

RESCUE

Mountain rescue in the Alps is probably the best in the world. So if you have the misfortune to ever need it, you know you are getting the best.

It is professional, i.e. the team members are paid and in many cases they are full-time mountain rescuers. This means that sometimes (not always) a charge is made. Therefore you must be insured.

SUMMONING HELP

The Alpine Distress Signal - any visible or audible signal made 6 times in a minute, e.g. torch flashes, whistle blasts, waving something etc.

The reply - three such signals made in a minute, meaning that the message has been understood.

By telephone - currently

Switzerland	General Rescue Number 117
	Sion Police 027 72 56 56
	REGA 01 383 11 11
France	General Rescue Number 112
	P.G.H.M. Chamonix 04 50 53 16 89
Italy	General Rescue Number 113
Austria	Police General Number 133
	Mountain Rescue 05222 22122, 194, 27777

These numbers are usually on maps and guidebooks. Mountain huts are always equipped with radio telephones and many climbers (e.g. guides) carry a mobile telephone.

HELICOPTERS

Help is likely to come in the form of a helicopter and usually it will winch down a crewman who will decide what action to take. Your action is to:

i) - indicate to the helicopter by standing with both arms raised above your head.

IF YOU WANT HELP, STAND WITH BOTH ARMS RAISED ABOVE THE HEAD.

IF YOU DO NOT WANT HELP, STAND WITH ONE ARM RAISED ABOVE THE HEAD AND THE OTHER DOWNWARDS.

ii) - make sure that all loose objects (polybags, bivvy shelters, hats etc.) are removed and securely put away, as they may otherwise be sucked into the helicopter's engines.

iii) - if on steep ground, prepare an anchor point for the crewman with a karabiner attached, and offer this to him.

iv) - only approach the helicopter from in front and ONLY on a signal from the pilot.

INSURANCE CERTIFICATES

There are stories about helicopters refusing to take casualties who do not have their Insurance Certificates with them. I have found no evidence to support these stories, but it will certainly make life easier when you get to the hospital if you have your Certificate with you.

HOSPITAL

If you are in France or other EEC country, part of the hospital bill will be covered by the EEC Reciprocal Agreement and part will fall to your insurance. It may be that Europe Assistance will take care of it, as they are used to these things and are most helpful. But it may be that you will be required to:

- produce a Form E111 which you get in advance from your post office.

- before leaving the hospital, pay the balance which falls to your insurance, and you recover this later from the insurance company.

SAFETY

Safety is not bought in by buying every piece of safety equipment. All that guarantees is that eventually you will have to use it. Your rucsack will be so heavy that you will be unable to go at guidebook time and you will end up having some kind of drama. But you will have your safety equipment.....

Safety is: good personal skills plus sound decision making.

PERSONAL SKILLS

The skills which need to be mastered are:

- good footwork with and without crampons.

- the art of moving together.

- selection of direct belays.

- route finding on a long route.

- crevasse identification and choice of route on a glacier.

- quick but safe abseiling.

- understanding the weather.

- generally going at guidebook time.

SOUND DECISION MAKING

To be sound, decisions must be realistic. And the main ones to be made will be on:

- the choice of route.
- the weather.

SAFETY EQUIPMENT

What you carry is a matter of personal choice, but I recommend that it is kept to a minimum, for example:

Bivouac bag - a group shelter is light and compact, and is a proven lifesaver. It has the advantage over individual bags of getting the group together to share body warmth and companionship in this disagreeable situation. Poly bags are next to useless as they are bad for condensation and the wind can get in through the top.

First Aid - minimal. (See 'First Aid').

Crampon Repair Kit - a few bits of wire and tape, and a couple of nuts and bolts.

SNOW AND ICE BELAYS

The most usual times for using a belay in snow or ice are:

- crossing bergschrunds.

- on steep snow or ice as part of a route.

- crevasse rescue.

A SELECTION OF BELAYS

Snow and ice belays are not as strong as rock belays and it must be stressed that snow belays in particular need to be practised time and again, in order to understand how snow varies.

The following selection should cover most situations:

Vertical Axe

In summer the snow is usually well consolidated and strong, especially if it is freezing. Often there are frozen slots where other people have placed their axes.

- push the axe in vertically, preferably into a frozen slot, right up to the head of the axe.

- put the rope behind the axe

- place one hand on top of the axe and try to transmit as much body weight as possible onto the top of the axe. This is essential.

- take the rope in with the spare hand. A third hand would be useful here, but as we don't have one it means letting go occasionally of the rope. It is vital to always keep one hand on the top of the axe, with your body weight on it.

Snow Bollard

The strength of the bollard or mushroom is not determined so much by its size, but by the strength of the various snow layers. It requires experience gained from much practice to construct one safely, as is the case with all snow belays.

- in good snow a bollard of 18" diameter will be quick to make and will be strong enough. A depth of 6"-9" may be enough, but the important point is to get the rope behind a strong layer of snow - however far down that is.

- angle the back wall at 90° less 10°-15°, as with all snow and ice belays.

- do not bring the channels in towards each other as in so doing you will isolate the bollard and weaken it.

- the bollard can be reinforced by placing ice axes at its ears. When abseiling, the last person brings the axes with him - so this is maybe an occasion to volunteer to go first. All things being equal, it makes sense for the lightest to come down last.

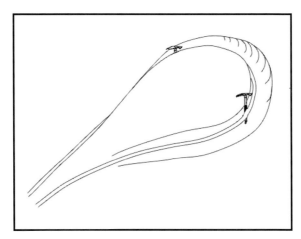

A SNOW BOLLARD

Horizontally Buried Axe

In strong snow this is an excellent anchor, but do not use a wooden shafted axe as it might break.

- CUT A SLOT JUST LONGER THAN THE AXE AND AT RIGHT ANGLES TO THE PREDICTED LINE OF PULL.

- SHAPE THE FRONT WALL: 90° LESS 10°-15°.

-CUT A SLOT FOR THE SLING AND ROPE, BEING CAREFUL NOT TO DAMAGE THE FRONT WALL AND ALSO ENSURING THAT THE SLOT IS DOWN TO THE SAME DEPTH AS THE AXE.

- ATTACH A SLING + SCREWGATE TO THE AXE WITH A CLOVE HITCH, AND DROP THE AXE INTO THE SLOT.

- AN OPTION IS TO FURTHER STRENGTHEN IT BY PLACING A SECOND AXE VERTICALLY IN FRONT OF THE HORIZONTAL ONE: A REINFORCED BURIED AXE BELAY.

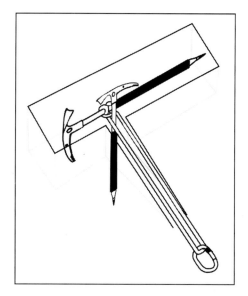

Ice Screws

The main types are: screw-in and drive-in. The drive-in are quicker to place but screw-ins are stronger. And the fatter, the stronger.

Two good ones are usual for a main belay.

AS WITH ALL SNOW AND ICE BELAYS, PLACE THE SCREW AT 90° LESS 10°-15°.

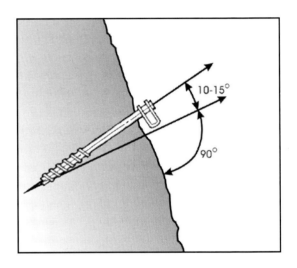

LINK THEM IN SUCH A WAY THAT THE PULL COMES EQUALLY ON EACH SCREW AND THE ANGLE BETWEEN EACH SCREW IS AS NARROW AS POSSIBLE - CERTAINLY LESS THAN 90°.

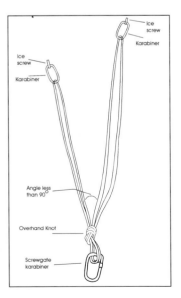

WHEN TO USE SNOW/ICE BELAYS

Bergschrunds

IN ASCENT - The bergschrund will be above you, so the leader is protected by the weight of the rest of the party being downhill. They do not take a belay or stance, but simply keep the rope reasonably tight. If the leader goes in, their weight combined with the friction of the rope on the lip will be enough.

Belaying the rope round the body or taking other belays just takes time, probably complicates the issue, and does not contribute greatly to holding the fall.

The leader uses a vertical axe to bring up the next person.

IN DESCENT - if the bridge looks good, the above procedure is used in reverse with people being protected in turn by a vertical axe above. If the bridge looks weak but the bergschrund is narrow - jump over it.

If the bridge looks weak or is non-existent, or if the bergschrund is too wide to jump, it will be best to abseil over it using a snow bollard.

On Steep Snow or Ice

SNOW - Remember that the guidebook time will assume that you move together on steep snow. If neither of you feels up to that, it is maybe time to go home. A vertical axe is usually good enough to bring up a second - if the snow is not good enough for one, it probably means it is too soft and you should get off it.

ICE - For a main belay usually use 2 screws. For runners use a single screw clipped with a quick draw.

Crevasse Rescue

If there is enough snow, the main anchor should be a horizontally buried axe. If there is not enough snow for that, clear away the ice and use 2 screws.

For techniques of rescue, see 'Crevasse Rescue'.

"Hold on a minute while I jump into this crevasse. I want to see if I can remember what I read in that book..."

SUN PROTECTION

TYPES OF LIGHT

Light consists of three main wavelengths:

Short Wave: ultra violet (UV) which is further subdivided according to the length of the wave:

- UVA is the longest and tans the skin.

- UVB is in the middle and causes sunburn.

- UVC is the shortest, is mainly absorbed by the ozone layer, and is the most dangerous.

Not only can UV cause sunburn but it can also cause permanent damage to the eyes. There is more UV at altitude than at sea level, but what is important to realise is that it is reflected off snow and is present even on cloudy days.

Medium Wave: visible light (VL). Unlike UV and infrared, the brain is aware of VL. It is the light which makes us screw up our eyes.

Long Wave: Infrared (R) light. These rays act through the heat they give off. In extreme cases the eye could be damaged, although the eye is good at absorbing R rays - as is snow.

SUN GLASSES

It is essential to protect the eyes against UV light by always wearing sun glasses on snow, even on cloudy days. Any lenses will absorb or reflect UV to some degree; so if you lose your good mountain dark glasses, wear anything over the eyes - even the plastic bag you keep the map in.

Good mountain glasses should:

- absorb or reflect 98%-100% UV.

- offer side protection.

- should fit well around the nose and against the cheeks for protection against rays which are reflected off the snow.

SUN CREAM

Factor Number - this multiplies the normal protection of the skin by the factor, i.e. with a Factor 10 you can theoretically stay out 10 times longer than without it.

Block - to me this seems a bit of a misnomer. The only effective block would be a suit of concrete.

Most suncreams offer protection against UVA and UVB, but few UVC. You can by a cream with a Factor 25 offering UVA, UVB and UVC protection; and another of Block 45 offering only UVA and UVB.

Beware relying on one application of Factor 45 at the start of the day - you might miss a crucial bit of skin or the cream might get rubbed off. Better to use a lower Factor and re-apply it often.

> **TOP TIP: always wear sunglasses on snow, even on cloudy days.**

WEATHER

Everyone knows that Weather Reports can go for days being very accurate, and then they go way off course. It is notoriously difficult to forecast the weather accurately, but by developing a knowledge of the weather you will increase your success rate on routes and you will reduce the chances of being caught in a storm. By 'knowledge of the weather' I mean two thing - the ability to understand a Weather Report, and the ability to observe what is happening around you.

The Alps are dominated by a maritime weather system, just like the British Isles, with Atlantic depressions and the Azores High being the main players.

MAIN WEATHER SYSTEMS

There are six main weather systems in the Alps.

1. Depressions - Low pressure

Atlantic Depressions are areas of low pressure which form out in the Atlantic. They generally move NE at an average speed of 25 knots with their centres crossing the British Isles.

They have sectors of warm and cold air. The usual progression is: a Warm Front, the warm sector, a Cold Front, the cold sector. If the Cold Front has caught up with the Warm Front, it is called an Occluded Front.

Depressions bring in quick changes in the weather. In the summer it is likely to be cooler than normal, while in the winter it is likely to be warmer. Much will depend on where the centre passes, but the best of the weather is likely to be in the south.

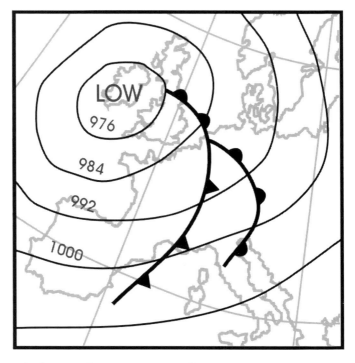

AN ATLANTIC DEPRESSION CROSSING BRITAIN WITH FRONTS TRAILING
OVER THE ALPS.

Effects on the Alps - Most depressions pass will to the north of the Alps. Typically the warm front hardly touches the Alps, but the trailing end of the cold front extends further south and brings a definite change in the weather.

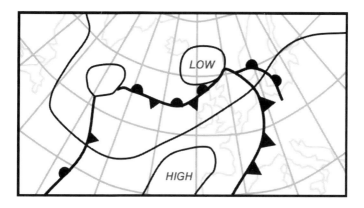

A cold front like this at the beginning or the end of the summer (early June or early September) will almost definitely bring rain and snow to the Alps with snow falling down to around 2,500m. Once the depression centered to the north of Britain has moved off, together with the cold front, it is possible that the Azores High will drift eastwards. If that happens, the Alps can expect a reasonable period of fine and settled weather.

2. Anticyclones - High pressure

In summer this is the Azores High. When established it keeps the Atlantic Depressions out by pushing them to the north and it tends to give long spells of fine settled weather - 'Le Grand Beau' in French. There may be some build up of cumulus cloud in the afternoon, which can develop into thunderstorms; but this is usually kept away by the quite strong valley and mountain winds associated with this weather system - see 'Fine Weather Winds' below.

High pressure often becomes established at the beginning of September. Since the sun is lower and the ground does not heat up so much, the local valley and mountain winds are not so strong, which is why this period can be one of the best times to go to the Alps.

In winter high pressure is usually due to the East European High which is created by cooling of the European continent. Although it may be sunny and clear up on the mountains, the valleys are often humid and foggy with frequent valley inversions.

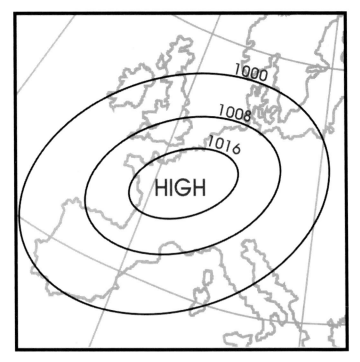

AN ANTICYCLONE AFFECTING THE ALPS

3. Weak pressure gradient

Quite often in summer we get a weak pressure system.

Weak pressure means weak winds, which in turn means that the air next to the ground can warm up. This results in a build up of cumulus and a risk of thunderstorms in the late afternoon or early evening. The clouds break up at sunset as the temperature drops to give a clear night.

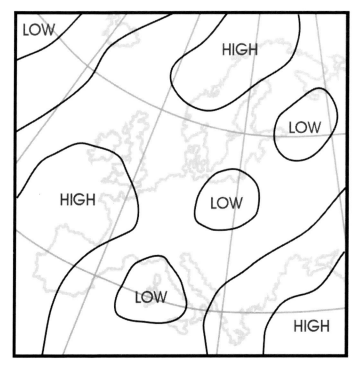

A WEAK PRESSURE GRADIENT

4. Föhn

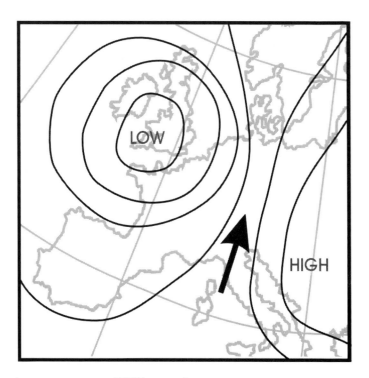

A DEPRESSION TO THE N/NW OF THE ALPS BRINGS WARM MOIST AIR UP FROM
THE MEDITERRANEAN, MAYBE EVEN WITH SAND FROM THE SAHARA.

The result of this air meeting the Alps is:

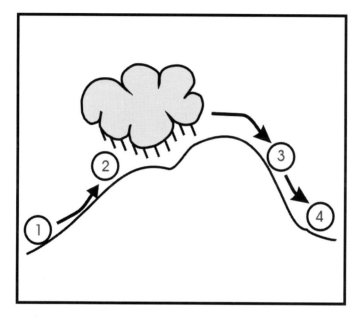

(1) IT COOLS AT 1°C PER 200M
(2) RAIN OR SNOW
(3) IT WARMS AT 1°C PER 100M
(4) HOT AND DRY

Note the difference in the lapse rates between moist and dry air at (1) and (3).

The south and west Alps are likely to be wet and windy; while the north and east will be sunny and warm. And in the valleys affected by the föhn there will be strong and gusting winds.

5. Northern Föhn

With an Anticyclone over west Britain and a Depression over east Europe you get the exact opposite of the Föhn.

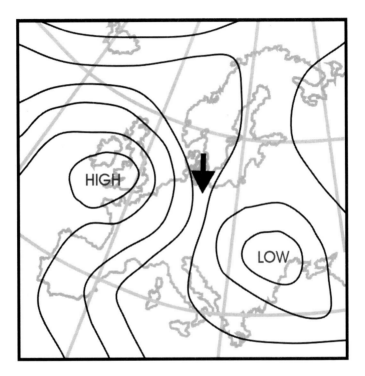

A cold wet wind hits the northern Alps bringing rain to the northern Alps, with the best of the weather in the southern Alps. In winter the north wind can bring very low temperatures; and if the wind is out of the NW rather than the N, the result is heavy snowfalls and avalanche conditions.

The likely development is that the Anticyclone will drift east, bringing better weather to the Alps. So this situation usually brings better weather, starting with the western Alps and spreading east.

6. Bise

The Bise is a dry continental wind coming in from Russia. The typical situation is an Anticyclone over northern Europe and a Depression over the Mediterranean.

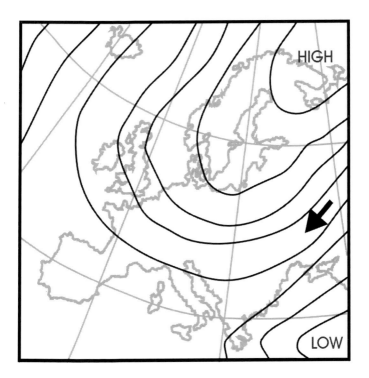

In winter the Bise is dry and cold, often with unpleasant cloud inversions and poor visibility due to the pollution from the east European industries.

In summer the wind is dry and warm, probably strongest between 1000m - 1500m, with the same poor visibility.

FINE WEATHER WINDS

In periods of fine settled weather, areas of ground are heated causing air to rise. This results in a difference in pressure between the warmer area and the cooler area, and the difference is balanced by a wind blowing from the cooler area to the warmer area. An important factor is that the fine weather is caused by a high pressure system.

There are two main ones:

Valley wind (Anabatic):

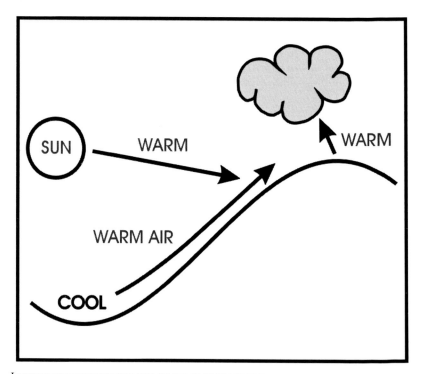

IN THE EARLY MORNING THE SUN STARTS TO WARM UP THE UPPER MOUNTAIN SLOPES WHILE THE VALLEY IS STILL IN THE SHADE. THE WARM AIR RISES CAUSING A LOCAL WIND TO BLOW FROM THE VALLEY UP THE MOUNTAIN.

Valley winds are not only very predictable in fine weather but are sometimes surprisingly strong. You only have to go to Martigny in the Rhône valley to see a good example.

Mountain Wind (Katabatic):

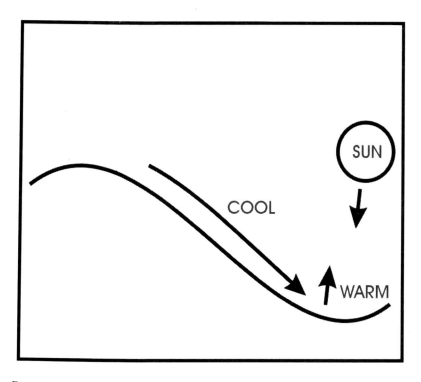

DURING THE DAY THE VALLEY WARMS UP AS THE SUN GETS OVERHEAD; AND THEN TOWARDS EVENING THE MOUNTAINS START TO COOL DOWN - QUICKER THAN THE VALLEY. WARM AIR RISES FROM THE VALLEY AND COOL AIR FLOWS DOWN FROM THE MOUNTAINS TO TAKE ITS PLACE.

The mountain wind is particularly noticeable just after sunset, but it is not as strong as the valley wind.

THUNDERSTORMS

A thunderstorm is one of the most serious dangers facing the Alpinist. It is dealt with in more detail in the chapter 'Lightning', while here are described the weather systems to watch for.

There are two systems:

Frontal system

The undercutting affect of a cold front causes rapid cooling of the air and very sudden thunderstorms. If you have been watching the weather forecasts, you should be aware of the front coming in. And then a noticeable drop in pressure is the imminent warning of these storms. By the time you notice the hooked cirrus, it is probably too late to get off the mountain. There will be a marked drop in temperature with severe showers of hail or snow, followed quickly by the thunder and lightning.

These storms mark a change in the weather and they are a great danger to the alpinist.

Hot Weather

These occur typically in summer between May and September with a weak pressure gradient system giving light winds, humidity and instability. During the day the ground is heated causing this warm and humid air to rise. The air feels heavy, and clouds form as *altocumulus castellanus* or *altocumulus flocus* followed by *cumulus*. When they finally flatten out into the anvil shape of *cumulonimbus*, the storm is ready and imminent.

By watching the cloud development, it is possible to predict these storms. They are very localised, and they generally do not last more than two hours. Apart from a temporary drop in temperature, they do not cause a major change in the weather. In fact, the next morning is invariably fine and sunny.